Come and Play

Little Ted's Big Adventure

ABC
Books

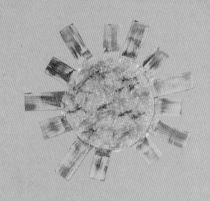

Little Ted, big adventure,
off into the day.

Up and down and all around,
now we're on our way.

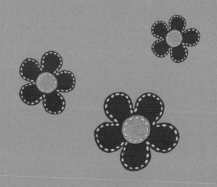

Little Ted, big adventure,
waving as we go.

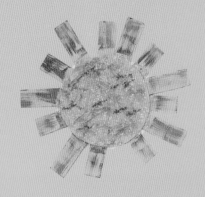

Moving through the world
as we travel to and fro.

Oh, oh, oh!
Here we go, go, go!
All the different ways
that we can move!

Little Ted, big adventure,
off into the blue.

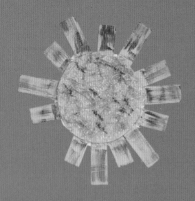

Every day's a big adventure,
when we explore the world
with you.